INFORMATION EXPLORER

SUPER SMART
INFORMATION
STRATEGIES

HIT THE BOOKS

*For Diane —
my WBB
and writing partner.
Happy reading!
with love
Suzy*

by Suzy Rabbat

CHERRY LAKE PUBLISHING • ANN ARBOR, MICHIGAN

CHERRY LAKE
Publishing

Published in the United States of America
by Cherry Lake Publishing
Ann Arbor, Michigan
www.cherrylakepublishing.com

Content Adviser: Gail Dickinson, PhD,
Associate Professor, Old Dominion University,
Norfolk, Virginia

Book design and illustration: The Design Lab

Photo credits: Cover and page 1, ©George Muresan, used under license from
Shutterstock, Inc.; pages 3, 7, 11, 15, 17, 23, 24, and 29, ©iStockphoto.com/
bluestocking; page 12, ©arenacreative, used under license from Shutterstock,
Inc.; page 21, ©wow, used under license from Shutterstock, Inc.; page 27,
©terekhov igor, used under license from Shutterstock, Inc.; page 28, ©sban,
used under license from Shutterstock, Inc.

Library of Congress Cataloging-in-Publication Data
Rabbat, Suzy.
    Super smart information strategies. Hit the books / by Suzy Rabbat.
        p. cm.—(Information explorer)
    Includes bibliographical references and index.
    ISBN-13: 978-1-60279-641-6   ISBN-10: 1-60279-641-6 (lib.bdg.)
    ISBN-13: 978-1-60279-649-2   ISBN-10: 1-60279-649-1 (pbk.)
    1. Research—Methodology—Juvenile literature. 2. Library
research—Juvenile literature. 3. Books—Juvenile literature. 4. Reference
books—Juvenile literature. 5. Information literacy—Juvenile literature.
I. Title. II. Title: Hit the books. III. Series.
    ZA3080.R33 2010   2009029512
    001.4'2—dc22

Cherry Lake Publishing would like to acknowledge the work
of The Partnership for 21st Century Skills. Please visit
www.21stcenturyskills.org for more information.

Printed in the United States of America
Corporate Graphics Inc.
January 2010
CLSP06

Table of Contents

CHAPTER ONE
Book Basics

Do you enjoy feasting on fiction?

Is your mind hungry? Books are like food for your brain. They help you understand the world around you. Some readers dine on fiction titles. They like to feast on stories that are creations of an author's imagination. To fully enjoy a fiction book, you need to read the entire story from cover to cover. The process is like eating an entire meal from appetizer to dessert.

Others enjoy reading nonfiction books. These books focus on facts, real events, and real people. Many people read nonfiction books for pleasure. But others use the information in these books for homework or projects. At times, you may be looking for one specific piece of information. In that case, you don't need to read an entire nonfiction book to find what you need. You don't need a whole meal when a snack will do! Let's learn how to make the most of nonfiction books and the information they contain.

Have you ever read the back of a cereal box to find out what was inside? You can also preview any book by taking a close look at the cover. The front cover usually shows the title and the names of the author and illustrator. The back cover may give a summary of the book.

What can you learn by reading the back of a cereal box?

Dust jackets are book covers. They often have information about the book printed on them.

It may also provide additional information about the author. Does the book have a dust jacket? You can usually find a summary of the book on the inside front flap. Information about the author is shown on the back flap.

A good nonfiction book has many built-in tools to help you find information quickly. One tool is the table of contents. Some books call this page "Contents." It includes a list of chapter titles followed by page numbers that show where each chapter begins. As you skim the chapter titles, think about the information you're trying to find. You may not find the exact words you're looking for in the contents. That's why it's a good idea to brainstorm some additional words that are related to your topic. Are any of those terms in the table of contents?

The index is a bit like the table of contents, but it gives more details about what you'll find in the book. It's a list of topics and keywords arranged in alphabetical order at the back of the book. There are page numbers next to each topic. They show you where to find each word in the text.

There are two other sections at the back of many books that provide helpful information: the glossary and bibliography. The glossary is like a dictionary. Words that readers may not understand often appear in bold print in the text. These words are listed in the glossary with their definitions. The bibliography leads you to other books and Web sites with additional information. The bibliography may be labeled "For More Information" or "Find Out More."

In this book the glossary words are highlighted in yellow.

The table of contents is on page 3. The index is on page 32.

Turn to page 30 to view the glossary and page 31 to see the bibliography.

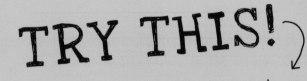

TRY THIS!

Take a close look at this book. What can you learn by examining the front and back covers? Flip through the pages. Skim the table of contents and index. Scan the glossary and bibliography. Do you have a better idea of what will be discussed throughout this book?

Reference books are nonfiction works that provide reliable information. They are often good places to begin your research when you want a general idea about your topic. They can also help you discover other ideas that are related to your project. Looking for big ideas and related topics can help shape your research and give you more to think about.

There are many different kinds of reference books. Each has something special to offer. Encyclopedias contain short articles about many topics.

Did you know that the dictionary is also a great tool for research? When you read the definition of specific words from your topic, you may come across other words that are related to your project. Use these words as search terms to find other helpful books or Web sites.

An atlas is a book of maps. Some atlases contain maps of just one country. An atlas of the world has maps of every country and the oceans.

Almanacs are filled with thousands of facts about many subjects. Many of these facts change over time. That is why almanacs are usually published each year.

Almanacs are filled with all kinds of interesting information.

THE OLD FARMERS 2009 ALMANAC
WEATHER

DID YOU KNOW THIS?

Benjamin Franklin started publishing Poor Richard's Almanack in the early 1730s. He wrote the almanac under a different name: Richard Saunders. People turned to Poor Richard's Almanack for information about weather and everyday advice. Would you like to learn more about Franklin and Poor Richard's Almanack? What kinds of nonfiction books could you use to find more information?

Each library has its own rules for using reference books. Many times, the reference books are kept in a special area. Some libraries keep them with the nonfiction collection. At most libraries, people are allowed to use the reference books at home. Explore your local library. Find the reference books. Ask your librarian if these books can be checked out. Browse the titles. Make note of the ones that may be useful for school projects.

There are records of every book in the library. These records are stored in the library catalog. Each record has information about one book. Most libraries have electronic catalogs. They allow you to search for books by subject, title, or author. This electronic catalog is called the Online Public Access Catalog (OPAC). You can access the OPAC from a computer station within the library. You can also access it online from your home computer. Each library's OPAC may look slightly different on your computer monitor. Pretend you're looking for a book about insects. Type insects in the search field to search by keyword. The search results display a list of book titles about insects along with their call numbers. A call number is like a code with letters or a combination of letters and numbers. It is used to help you locate items in the library. The call number is found on the spine of the book.

What are the call numbers for these books?

Did you Know this ?

HERE ARE SOME TIPS FOR USING THE OPAC:
- Capital letters are not needed for search terms.
- Be sure your search terms are spelled correctly.
- Does the title begin with A, An, or The? Drop those words and start your search with the next word in the title. To search for The Amazing Book of Spiders, for example, just type amazing book of spiders.
- To search by author, start with the author's last name followed by a comma and the author's first name. To search for Mary Smith, your entry would look like this: smith, mary.

When you search for specific subjects, you will find that most of the books in your results have similar call numbers. The call number for books about insects is 595.7. This gives a general idea of where to look for insect books. To find these books on the shelf, start in the nonfiction section of the library. Check the shelf signs to find books with call numbers in the 500s. Stop when you find the right aisle. Read the call number on any book. Compare it to the call number you're looking

Signs at the end of each row of books will help you find the row with the call numbers you need.

for. If your call number is higher than what you see on the books, keep walking. If it's lower, back up. You may have to check the numbers on the shelves several times before finding the right books!

TRY THIS!

Think of a sport or activity you'd like to know more about. Snowboarding, lacrosse, and yoga are a few examples.

1. Type the activity keyword in the search field of your library's OPAC. Take a close look at the results. What do you notice about the call numbers? Do the books about specific subjects have similar numbers? Could that mean they are grouped together?

2. Pick three nonfiction books on the activity you chose. Write down their titles and call numbers.

3. Head over to the nonfiction area of the library. Locate the books on your list.

4. Look at the other titles in that section of the shelves. Do you see more books that might help you better understand your topic?

CHAPTER TWO
Finding the Right Book

Your search for information doesn't stop here. Finding books about your topic is a good start. But before you decide which books to use, take a closer look. Be picky! Take the time to find the best information source to fit your needs. Have you ever shopped for a coat? If so, you know there's more to finding the perfect coat than choosing one that fits. You need to think about the weather in your area. You should also consider the price and different styles. Be just as selective when you pick books.

You have to consider many things when buying a coat. You should also be picky about the books you choose for a project!

Finding the right book can make your research successful. Here are some things to think about as you select a nonfiction book:

- ✓ **Information:** Do the facts and ideas in the chapters help answer your questions? Use the table of contents and index to discover what's inside the book.

- ✓ **Authority:** What is the author's background? Is this person an expert? Does she have special knowledge about the subject? This can help you determine how reliable the information is.

- ✓ **Readability:** Is the text too advanced? Too simple? Open the book to any chapter. Read a page or two. Do you understand what you've read? Can you restate the main ideas in your own words?

- ✓ **Ease of Use:** Is the book organized? Can you quickly find what you need? Return to the table of contents and index. Also, look for headings and subheadings in the text. Special fonts or bold print are helpful, too.

- ✓ **Pictures and Diagrams:** Are there illustrations or charts? Do they help you understand the topic?

- ✓ **Currency:** Does the book have up-to-date information? Check the year of publication.

TRY THIS!

Take the three books you selected on the sport or activity of your choice. Evaluate them using the points listed on page 15.

Before you start, think about your reasons for using the books. Do you want to know more about the rules of the activity? Are you interested in learning about its history? Thinking about your purpose helps you spot keywords or related terms in the table of contents and index. Are you just curious about the activity in general? Look for information that interests you.

Make a chart like the one on the next page to help organize your thoughts. Rate each aspect of the book using a number scale of 1 to 5. A score of 1 means "poor" and 5 means "excellent." The sample chart is filled out to help you better understand the rating system. It evaluates how useful three books on spiders would be for a project about tarantulas.

continued ⟶

Book Evaluation Chart

	BOOK A	BOOK B	BOOK C
Information	3—there is not a lot of specific information on tarantulas	5—covers all kinds of spiders with several chapters on tarantulas	3—text does not offer a lot of details
Authority	3—the author collects spiders as a hobby	5 – the author is a scientist who studies tarantulas	2—the author does not have much experience with spiders
Readability	2—text is too advanced	5—vocabulary and concepts are easy to understand	2—text is too simple
Ease of Use	4—there are helpful headings in the text	4—the text layout is easy to follow	1—there is no index
Pictures and Diagrams	3—has some interesting illustrations	4—has excellent color photos	2—doesn't have many photographs or drawings
Currency	3 —published during the 1990s	4—published within the last 2 years	2—published during the 1980s
TOTAL SCORE	18	27	12

Which book got the highest rating? Chances are that book would be a good resource for your project. Don't automatically toss aside the other titles. They may offer some helpful information, too.

Give it a try. Which book on your list got the highest score? It is probably the best fit for your information needs. That book should be your top pick.

CHAPTER THREE
Reading for Understanding

You probably wouldn't eat soup with a fork or cut an apple with a spoon. You use different tools to eat different foods. It's the same when reading. You need different reading skills and tools to digest or understand different kinds of writing. Reading to understand

Choosing the wrong tool for a job can lead to big problems!

The table of contents is like a menu for your book. Which chapter will feed your information need?

information is a little like eating slowly to really enjoy each bite. Here is a checklist of things to keep in mind as you read:

☑ **Check out the menu.** Begin with the table of contents or index. Zoom in on the information you need.

☑ **Take small bites.** Read the text in "chunks." Take in a few paragraphs at a time. Stop and ask yourself, "Do I understand what I've read? Can I paraphrase this information by stating it in my own words?"

☑ **Chew on the new facts.** Think about new ideas in relation to what you already know about the topic. Do they agree with your background knowledge? It's always a good idea to check information you find against additional books or Web sites.

Don't forget to check out the illustrations and captions in books. They might be full of tasty bits of information!

☑ **Don't forget the condiments.** Salt or ketchup add flavor to food. In the same way, the illustrations and diagrams in a book add meaning to the words. Don't forget to read the captions near any images.

☑ **Check the ingredients.** A glossary is like a list of ingredients, except that all of the ingredients are words that appear in what you are reading. Just as you need to know what the ingredients are when you prepare a meal, you need to understand the words that are used in order to understand what you are reading. Turn to the glossary for help with unfamiliar words.

TRY THIS!

Take a closer look at the sport or activity book you selected as your top pick. Choose a chapter from the table of contents. Now practice all of the strategies in the checklist. Focus on carefully reading small sections of text at a time. Can you paraphrase the main ideas? Practice with a friend or family member. Read a paragraph or two. Then, in your own words, teach the other person the information you just learned. Repeat the process until you get through an entire chapter.

Practicing your reading and research skills with friends can help you become an information expert.

CHAPTER FOUR

Using Information Responsibly

Pretend your neighbor left his bike on the driveway.
It wouldn't be right for you to take it. The bike is your
neighbor's property. In a similar way, you cannot use
an author's words in your research assignment as if
they were your own. It's like taking something that
doesn't belong to you. Information that is published in

Don't be an information thief! Be sure to cite your sources.

THIEF!

books is the intellectual property of the author or publisher. You can use what you've learned by paraphras-
ing the information. If you do use the author's exact
words, put quotation marks around the text. Write
a citation to show where you found the information.
Other people will then know where to look to check
your facts or find out more.

When it's time to cite your source, the title page and
copyright page have everything you need. The title page
lists the title of the book. You'll also find the names of
the author and publishing company. The copyright page
is usually found on the back of the title page. There,
you'll find the date when the book was published. The
date of publication may be important, depending on
your topic. If you are reading about how to hard boil an
egg, for example, this date is not critical. The information on this topic doesn't really change over time. But
scientists are making new discoveries every day. So
if you're looking for data about a topic such as space
travel, you want up-to-date information.

In this book, the
copyright information
is on page 2.

TRY THIS!

There are different ways to record citations. Ask a teacher or librarian for help if you need it.

21st Century Skills **INNOVATION** *Library*

Vision

by Susan H. Gray

INNOVATION IN   MEDICINE

Here's one way to write a citation for a book:

A CITATION LOOKS LIKE THIS:

Gray, Susan H. *Vision*. Ann Arbor, MI: Cherry Lake Publishing, 2009.

DON'T FORGET THESE ELEMENTS IN YOUR CITATION:

- AUTHOR'S NAME: Susan H. Gray
- TITLE: *Vision*
- CITY OF PUBLICATION: Ann Arbor
- PUBLISHER: Cherry Lake Publishing
- DATE OF PUBLICATION: 2009

continued ⟶

Published in the United States of America by Cherry Lake Publishing
Ann Arbor, Michigan
www.cherrylakepublishing.com

Content Adviser: Noshene Ranjbar, MD

Design: The Design Lab

Photo Credits: Cover and page 3, ©iStockphoto.com/johncl; page 4, ©Blend Images/Alamy; page 7,
©North Wind Picture Archives/Alamy; page 8, ©Corbis Premium RF/Alamy; page 11, ©INTERFOTO
Pressebildagentur/Alamy; page 14, ©iStockphoto.com/davex83; page 15, ©Judy Drietz, used under
license from Shutterstock, Inc.; page 17, ©iStockphoto.com/dlewis33; page 18, ©PHOTOTAKE Inc./
Alamy; pages 20 and 21, ©Medical-on-Line/Alamy; page 23, ©PhotoCreate, used under license from
Shutterstock, Inc.; page 24, ©Exotic eye/Alamy; page 26, ©Lisa F. Young, used under license from
Shutterstock, Inc.; page 27, ©Christine Osborne Pictures/Alamy; page 28, ©Suzanne Porter/Alamy

Library of Congress Cataloging-in-Publication Data
Gray, Susan H., 1954–
Vision / by Susan H. Gray.
  p. cm.–(Innovation in medicine)
Includes index.
ISBN-13: 978-1-60279-226-5
ISBN-10: 1-60279-226-7
1. Vision disorders–Treatment–Technological innovations–Juvenile
literature. 2. Vision–Juvenile literature. 3. Ophthalmic
lenses–History–Juvenile literature. I. Title. II. Series.
RE91.G63 2009
617.7–dc22   2008006753

Cherry Lake Publishing would like to acknowledge the work of
                                             ation.

TRY THIS! (CONTINUED)

Now try it yourself. Practice citing your sources. Choose three nonfiction books on any topic that interests you. Look at the title and copyright pages. Find all of the information you need to cite those sources. Write down your citations.

Often the information you need for citing a book can be found on the title and copyright pages.

Turn to page 31 and look at the Find Out Mores section of this book to see more examples of citations.

CHAPTER FIVE

E-books and More

Electronic books, or e-books, are like the paper books you use most of the time. But the information they contain is presented in a different form. Nonfiction e-books have the same features as the nonfiction books in the library. They're organized the same way, too. You should evaluate them as you would any print resource.

Many libraries offer e-books for people to borrow. You can visit your library's Web site from a home computer. You use your library card to check out e-books. When you check out an ebook, the file is downloaded to your computer. You can then read it on your computer monitor. You can return the book with a click of your mouse. Even if you don't return it, the book will simply stop working after its due date.

There are other advantages to using e-books. You can search through the text to find specific words. You can often change the font size to make the words easier to read. You may be able to highlight important parts of the text and add a digital bookmark to save your place.

You can also purchase e-books online. When you buy an e-book, the file is downloaded to your computer. You can also download files to a portable e-book device, or e-reader.

TRY THIS!

Does your local library offer e-books? Visit its Web site and find out. If so, browse your options. Find a nonfiction title that interests you. Follow the directions on the site and download the file to your computer. If your library does not have e-book collections, try a different site. Ask an adult to help you find Web sites that offer e-books for children. One option is Barnes & Noble (www.barnesandnoble.com). Keep in mind that prices vary for different e-books on different sites. You may also need to download special software to read the e-books. Never download anything without an adult's permission. Once you have selected a title, start reading! Explore the different features of the e-book. Come up with three ways that e-books are different from printed books.

You won't need to lug around a heavy stack of books if you use an e-reader!

You can store hundreds of books on a laptop or e-reader. You can also use a personal digital assistant (PDA). Carrying around a device full of files is much easier than carrying a heavy stack of books.

Okay, smart searchers! You've practiced some great strategies for using nonfiction books. You know how to select and evaluate books that fit your needs. You also know how to use tools to locate information quickly. Have fun filling up on the information that good nonfiction books provide. *Bon appétit!*

Downloading books to an e-reader is quick and easy.

Nonfiction Checklist

Here is a reminder of points to think about as you use nonfiction books:

1. What questions do I have about my topic?
2. How can I use the OPAC to find nonfiction books at my library?
3. What should I look for when I'm evaluating nonfiction books?
4. What strategies are best for reading nonfiction?
5. Did I create citations to give credit to the authors?
6. Do these books have enough information to answer my questions?
7. Are there other good resources I can explore for more information?
8. Should I do anything different the next time I search for information?

Glossary

almanacs (AWL-muh-nakss) books published each year with information about many subjects

bibliography (bib-lee-OG-ruh-fee) a list of writings about a subject or by one author

bold print (BOHLD PRINT) text that is printed with thick, dark letters so that it stands out on the page

citation (sye-TAY-shuhn) the act or instance of giving credit to the source of a fact, quote, or other information

dust jacket (DUHST JAK-it) a removable paper cover that wraps around a book

glossary (GLOSS-uh-ree) an alphabetical list of difficult words and their meanings in a book

index (IN-dekss) an alphabetical list of topics in a book with page numbers showing where they are found in the text

intellectual property (in-tuh-LEK-choo-uhl PROP-ur-tee) an idea, invention, written work, or other creation of the mind that often has the potential to make money

keywords (KEE-wurdz) important words

paraphrase (PA-ruh-fraze) state information again in different words

spine (SPINE) the part of a book to which the pages are attached

table of contents (TAY-buhl UHV KON-tents) a list found at the beginning of a book with chapter titles and the page numbers on which they begin

Find Out More

BOOKS

Hamilton, John. *Books*. Edina, MN: ABDO Publishing Company, 2005.

Hamilton, John. *Libraries and Reference Materials*. Edina, MN: ABDO Publishing Company, 2005.

Orr, Tamra B. *Extraordinary Research Projects*. New York: Franklin Watts, 2006.

WEB SITES

Denver Public Library—Dewey Decimal Guide

kids.denverlibrary.org/ask/dewey.html

Find out more about one way that library books are organized.

KidsHealth—What Is Plagiarism?

kidshealth.org/kid/feeling/school/plagiarism.html

Learn more about why it is important to put information in your own words and cite your sources.

ReadWriteThink—Hints About Print

www.readwritethink.org/materials/hints-on-print/index.html

Follow an online tutorial on selecting nonfiction books and find a helpful evaluation guide.

Index

About the Author

Suzy Rabbat is a National Board certified school librarian. She has two children, Mike and Annie. She lives in Mt. Prospect, Illinois, with her husband, Basile.